The Waitress Book

51 Tips to Help You Double Yours

To Cindy,
    Thank you so much for
your support! In fact if all
people were more like you there
would have been no need to
write this book at all!

Joel Brown

JOEL BROWN

To Cindy,

Thank you so much for your support! If that it all people were more like you, there would have been no need to write this book at all!

Joel Brown

ISBN-13: 978-1542330428
ISBN-10: 1542330424

The Menu

::Appetizers::

WHY I WROTE THIS BOOK

Whet your appetite with this nostalgic memory of our author that led to the motivation to write this book **FOR WAITRESSES ONLY!**

|1|

BRAVEHEART

This teasing bit of movie lore will put you in the right frame of mind and awaken your hunger for our entrees that follow!

|3|

::Entrees::

IT'S ALL ABOUT ME

This toasty little special sets the table for every delicious tip that follows! And guess what? They have nothing to do with the customers; they are all about me. And by *me*, I mean **YOU!** Digest this entrée of 10 Tips, and this book will fill you up in every way. Oh yeah, check out the story of the $200 tip.

|5|

CINDERELLA MAN

This sizzling meal is our best seller. These 12 Tips are the meat and potatoes of the book. It's all about food. And note: All these tips come from personal experience.

|17|

THE SECRET TO MEN

A naughty and decadent plate on which I serve up the truth about MEN. With these 15 Tips, I take you inside the heart, mind, and wallet of men. This meal will not only help you make more tips from men, but it may improve your love life, too. It's everything you wanted to know about men but didn't know to ask.

|27|

::Side Orders::

Lots of assorted morsels of tips and secrets are shared on this platter. These dishes are imported from the best waitresses in the world. Enjoy!

|39|

::Dessert::

The Awesome Power of a Waitress. Yes, this is the only dessert we offer. It's sweet but strong. It's the delightful story of how a waitress's words inspired the writing of this book. You'll like it!

|45|

::Drinks::

First cup of coffee: Rich and cozy almost last words.

|47|

Last cup of coffee: Robust and lasting last words!

|49|

Why I Wrote This Book

Let's face it; there are not a lot of books written exclusively to and for waitresses. Publishers take off running at the mention of this book's title alone. So, why did I choose to write it? Because I love waitresses. I always have.

It all started the summer I turned 15 when a good friend of mine got a job washing dishes at the Waffle Hut in Gulf Shores, Alabama. It was there that I developed a crush on a 15-year-old blonde waitress named Susan. God, she was beautiful! Oh, you guessed it, I never asked her out. In fact, due to my adolescent shyness, I probably never even spoke to her. But I still think of her some 40 years later.

Since then I have met countless waitresses. Some of you I have laughed and joked with. Some of you I have cried and prayed with. For a few, I have put a coin in the jukebox so I could dance with you. And yes, some of you, much like that beautiful 15-year-old blonde in the Waffle Hut, I have fallen in love with.

This book was written out of true affection for all of the waitresses I've ever known, and even those I haven't. It's a result of a lifetime of getting to know you, watching you, listening to you, and asking you questions. I know it wasn't exactly normal to take such an interest; I never noticed any of my friends asking the waitresses the questions I did. I was always more interested in the life of my waitresses than the taste of my food. You see, I think people are far more interesting than roast beef or crab cakes. I find waitresses to be the most interesting of all!

I was shocked at how many waitresses I spoke to who were hurting for money, and many of them were even single moms. And you know as well as I do that $2.13 per hour doesn't cut it in this world we live in.

At the same time, I would meet some waitresses that were crushing it, even in small diners and cafes. Of course, I did my job and asked them their secrets. I would also ask them if they were trained on how to make big tips. The answer was always no. I finally realized the restaurant makes basically the same amount of money, regardless of how much their wait staff makes in tips, so it's none of their concern. But it is mine! I want all of you to make more money and live more successful lives, and I have written this book to prove it.

My goal with this book is to help you see that earning more money is completely within your power without ever getting a different job or getting that degree at night. I have degrees myself, but colleges don't teach you how to make money, they teach algebra, law, and literature. That will not pay your car note! I have seen the "tips" in this book used all over America to pad the pockets of successful waitresses, waiters, and bartenders. I believe with all of my heart and soul that they can help any waitress—and that includes you!

Braveheart

I know what you're thinking. You're wondering how someone like yourself can affect such a change that you could double your tips per year, maybe triple or even more.

In this book, I am going to reveal every secret I have ever been told on how waitresses make lots of money. If there were not great money to be had, bars and restaurants would be closing down all over the country. Americans love to eat out, and we love great food and great service, which leads to great dining experiences.

Now here is the deal. In almost every movie you have ever seen, from *Cinderella* to *King Kong*, there is a love story. And what happens in these movies? (And by the way they keep remaking them because they are so popular.) The man (or ape) goes through hell and back to find, keep, and protect his girl. Men love women and will fight for their safety and honor and freedom. That's how we are wired.

My favorite of these movies is *Braveheart* with Mel Gibson. It's the true story of William Wallace, a man in Scotland who falls in love with a beautiful maiden but then she is murdered by British soldiers. His crazy revenge of her death inspires a

3

whole land to fight and try to grasp their freedom. I am not asking any of you to inspire a man to revolution, or even get an ape to climb the Empire State building, but I am you asking to inspire your customers, both men and women, to tip you a little more—and sometimes it will be a lot more! How do you do this? What's the secret? The secret is: THEY WANT YOU TO INSPIRE THEM, to awe them, to wow them and to care about them. In fact, they are begging for it! They are dying for it! And guess what! They even tip for it!

ENTRÉE I

It's All About Me

Before we start the first tip, I ask that you think of Joan of Arc a 17-year-old peasant girl in France in the 15th century who convinced the leadership of her country to fight for their freedom and she led her people (men) into war and took their land and king back. She didn't even know how to fight or use a sword. But she did it! She believed she could!

My point, ladies, is that you have *untold power*. Think of all of the love songs written by guys about women, think of all the boats and yachts purchased to impress you guys. Think of all the new cars and trucks we buy every day, so we can be more attractive to you. Trust me; it's because of you that we wash our trucks or cut our hair or even get jobs and make money. Please know that your powers to influence us men are immeasurable.

And guess what? We want you to inspire us! Yes, we want you to. So let's get to it!

Here comes the first entrée of tips, and they all focus on you, the waitress. Thus, the name of this entrée, or section of the book, is "It's All About Me!"

Tip #1: Be the First to Smile

This tip is so simple that most waitresses forget to use it. It costs nothing and only takes a second. And its value is immense. If you only knew how a smile makes a man—or, for that matter, a women—feel. It helps us to feel accepted and wanted. It makes us feel happy. But smiling alone is not enough; you've got to be the one who smiles first. Don't let the customers greet you; that's *your* job. They may never have been there before and may be uncomfortable or even nervous. Welcome them with the first smile; you won't regret it!

"Anyone who stops learning is old, whether at twenty or eighty."

—Henry Ford

Tip #2: Welcome to Moe's

Smiling first is awesome, but if you want to supersize it, then speak first, too! When you make an effort to break the ice, even the shiest and most reserved customer can find their tongue. You're the host; it's your castle that the customer has entered. Start caring for them right off the bat, letting them know you're there to help. Start making them feel welcomed. When they relax and begin to talk, they will start enjoying you, and you will start enjoying them, too. As a result, they will feel more like tipping. I promise! Why do you think Firehouse Subs and Moe's Southwest Grill (two awesome places) requires employees to speak right when you crack open the door, "Welcome to Moe's!" It must be a good idea, right?

Tip #3: Your Opening Line

First, make sure your introductory line isn't, "You can sit anywhere you like" or "What can I get you to drink?" That's not enough to make you stand out or to make your customer feel comfortable or special. Be the awesome person you are, and put yourself in the customers' shoes. Perhaps they've had a hard day. Certainly, they're hungry, and you know how people can get when they are hungry. Try saying something warm and welcoming like, "How are you doing? We're so happy to have you today!" Or, "Wow, haven't seen you in a while!" or "Please come in!" or "Good morning (or evening)!" Pretend it's a friend that you haven't seen in a long time. Or how about this one, "We are so glad you chose (restaurant name) today! You'll love our food."

The most important part is your tone. Be personal and friendly, not mechanical. Hey, just be you. Your best you!

"Success is nothing more than a few disciplines practiced every day."

—Jim Rohn

Tip #4: Make Me Feel Important

As each customer walks into the restaurant, imagine that he or she is wearing a sign hanging around their neck that says: MAKE ME FEEL IMPORTANT!

Isn't that what all of us really want, anyway? To feel important, to feel noticed, to feel like we matter? In fact, we want that so much that we'll happily pay those who make us feel that way. Generosity grows from that place of feeling good about ourselves. A happy customer is a generous customer.

Of course you don't want to go overboard, and you don't want to be false or insincere. Show your customer, *in a genuine way*, that you appreciate him or her. This can be done by your smile or speaking first or even walking with them to the table. "So glad you came to my table or restaurant today."

If you master this tip and this tip alone, not only do you not need to read the rest of the book, but you will be successful in any and all areas of your life.

Tip #5: The Secret to Life

Yes, I know that's a big title. "The Secret to Life." Couldn't I have been a little more modest? I mean, really; are you kidding me? To *life*? Well, it's the secret I have used to create a wonderful life for myself. In fact, it's something I use every day, and it not only affects the people I use the secret on, but it is a two-edged sword because it also makes me happier and more positive as well.

Ready? It's very simple. In fact, you will probably disregard it as being *too* simple. But if there is one thing that I have learned, it is that all truth and wisdom is very simple. Here it is: Treat other people (your customers for this book) *better* than you want to be treated yourself. Not *as good* as you want to be treated, but better. In fact, all of these tips will somehow show you ways to fulfill this simple secret to life.

The simplest and easiest way to apply this to our situation is to find something about your customer to compliment them on and do it first. It can be anything—their hair, their shoes, their shirt, their watch, or even pictures of their grandchildren. But keep it honest; no false flattery! It won't work if you're lying.

"Flatter me, and I may not believe you. Criticize me, and I may not like you. Ignore me, and I may not forgive you. Encourage me, and I may not forget you."

—*William Arthur*

Tip #6: Name Tags Are So Money!

Let's lighten it up a little bit. This tip is easy, but it helps so much. Wear a name tag or, better yet, a uniform with your name on your shirt. It's also brilliant to put your hometown on it, especially if you're working at a tourist restaurant. Remember the waiters and waitresses at TGI Fridays? They used to wear tons of buttons and badges and blinking ornaments.

Any of these ideas will give your customer an easier way to connect with you. Adding a little personality to your outfit will help your customers feel warm and invited, and it also serves as a conversation starter. Remember, a relaxed, engaged customer is a tipping customer. Don't go against any of your restaurant rules, but hey, there are other ways to get the same results. I've seen waitresses use business cards with their name on them, which also works. Better yet, my favorite steakhouse has started using place cards with the waiter's name and the customers too!

Tip #7: There's No One Like You

Now here's a tip that applies not only to serving customers but also to life in general (and most especially in the area of female-to-male interaction). Ready? Here it is: Work with what the good Lord gave you! Believe me, you are a wonderful work of art, a true one of a kind. If you think that this doesn't apply to you because you were given nothing to work with, then you're wrong—dead wrong! Every woman has something beautiful or unique about her. It may be your eyes, your hair, your figure, that cute little dimple when you smile, or even your kindness or your sense of humor. (Take it from a man, a kind or happy woman is much more attractive than a "hot chick" with a cold heart.)

Your special attribute might be that you've already mastered many of the techniques in this book, and that's what sets you apart. Trust me, you have something. Now, it's up to you to discover what it is. Most of you have far more than one great asset. Don't let those treasures go untapped if you want to get tipped. Get out there and be you! Yes, you!

> *"God gives everyone certain attributes, characteristics, talents and then He says, 'If you use what you have, I'll increase it, but if you don't use it, you will lose it.' Use it or lose it; it's the law."*
>
> **—Charlie Tremendous Jones**

Tip #8: Who Loves You?

"Who Loves You" is the name of an old song by Frankie Valli Four Seasons. The lyrics ask the girl over and over, "Who loves you pretty baby? Who's always there to make it right?' Who in your restaurant loves you? Who is gonna help you make it right? Who is gonna make you successful? Not your fellow waitresses. Not your management. Not even the kitchen.

Yes, you want to work well with all of these people, but it's important to remember who's really got your back, who you're absolute *key* team members are. Who would that be? Your customers, of course!

Your boss isn't going to give you hour-by-hour raises for good work. Neither are your fellow waitresses or the kitchen. It's your customers who will do that for you. So return the favor, and look out for them. They're the ones with whom you need to start conversations, and they're the ones for whom you need to stand up and speak. "Hey, cook the soup is cold!" or "I told you to hold the bacon!" Take up for your customers. and we will love you for it. And tip you for it!

Tip #9: You Don't Need a Crystal Ball— But It Would Be Nice

I want to share with you what happens all too often in restaurants all over the land. Since its usually invisible, it's missed, ignored, and lost forever. Here's how it goes:

Someone calls one or more friends and says, "Hey, I got a cool new place to have lunch."

"Oh yeah? Tell me about it."

"Well, the food is fantastic, and the service is spot on…"

The date and time are set, and the moment comes when they all arrive at your restaurant excited and in a good mood. Perhaps they've even come to celebrate a birthday or a promotion.

Now, to the average waitress (which you are no longer), these customers look just like any other customers because the waitress hasn't seen or heard the phone calls or bragging about how great the food and service are. The waitress can't see the excitement that has been building for a week, nor can she know that someone in the group has bought a new skirt and someone else is wearing a brand new pair of shoes. The mood and expectations are high but are still invisible to the untrained eye. Help us out, crystal ball!

All of this leads us back to the reason that I consider the role of the waitress to be so important. You are given this invisible responsibility to either *wow* your customers or disappoint them. For an hour or so, you, the waitress, become the most important person in your customers' world. You unwittingly have the power to make or break this event for them. Yes, the

11

waitress is queen. You are the woman. Take charge! Make their day. How? Smile first, speak first, and you might even say:

- Are we celebrating something today?
- Is this your first time to dine with us?
- What a big crowd. Is this a special occasion?

Believe me, with every syllable you use you will increase their enjoyment and your tip. (Actually, there is no crystal ball required.)

Tip #10: Mind Your Own Business

Whether you work at a popsicle stand or a high-class restaurant, treat that place like it's yours. This will not only raise your tips, but it will get you promoted and get you raises.

Now, before you jump to any conclusions, let me clarify: I'm not talking about *Attitude* (with a capital A). I'm not talking about genuine pride and responsibility, just as an owner would have. Imagine now that you do own the restaurant or café where you work, and answer the following questions from that position as if you are the owner of the place:

- What time would you get there?
- Would you risk arriving late and missing potential customers?
- How late would you stay?
- Would you pick up those beer cans and cigarette butts in the parking lot?
- Would you dress differently or change how you do your hair?
- Would you ask with genuine interest how your customer is doing today? And remember his answer?

- Would you check that plate to see if the steak is rare like your customer ordered it?
- Would you move a little faster to get orders out to your customers?
- Would you try to engage your customers in a better eating experience?

Of course, you would do all of this and more because you would stand to make a lot of money if the business you own is successful. But, here's the thing, even without being the owner, you could make a lot more money by doing these very same things. Why? Because your customers will be so grateful that they will be dying to leave you bigger tips. They will also come back and eat there more often.

And your boss? He will notice the change in two seconds. And after he picks himself up off the floor, he will change the way he treats you. You will be his number one waitress. When you have a sick baby or a meeting with your child's teacher, you won't have to worry about losing your job. Your boss will say, "Honey, you just take your time."

In case you're not buying all of this, think of it this way: What makes someone a business owner? It's someone who, by her own efforts, stands to make better (or worse) money depending on how well she runs her business. Guess what? That's the definition of a waitress. You will make more (or less) money depending entirely on your own efforts. Being a waitress *is* your own business!

"The ability to deal with people is as purchasable a commodity as sugar or coffee, and I will pay more for that ability than for any other under the sun."

—John D. Rockefeller

The $200 Tip

I'm going to leave you with a story that sums up the essence of what this entrée is about.

It was date day for my wife, Rebekah, and me, and we loaded up our bikes and drove sixty miles to Pensacola Beach to enjoy a warm fall day and eat at one of my favorite restaurants, Peg Leg Pete's (they do it right!). Our waiter, Lewis, was a 51-year-old man who appeared to have had a stroke, leaving him with a slow-paced limp. But that didn't stop him from being a great waiter who used many of the tips this book offers. (And yes, he had a name tag on his shirt.)

He told us how great the grouper nuggets were and asked us if we were on vacation. Learning that we had our bikes with us, he gave us bike trail information that later led to a wonderful bike ride for Bek and me.

As we neared the end of our meal, Rebekah overheard a conversation between a customer (a middle-aged man like myself), his waitress, and our waiter, Lewis. Bek said it had something to do with "the nicest person working at Peg Leg's." At the end of this exchange, the customer gave Lewis something, shook his hand, and walked away. My curiosity took over; I had to know what had just transpired. When Lewis returned to our table, Bek asked him about it, explaining that we were not just being nosey, but that *"I was"* writing a book.

Lewis related the story. Apparently, the customer had asked his waitress, "Who is the nicest person working at Peg Leg Pete's?" and she had answered that it was him, Lewis. So, what had the customer given Lewis?

Lewis pulled out a fresh $100 bill from his pocket, and his eyes filled with tears. Yes, a 51-year-old man had tears rolling down his cheeks as he told us the story. He said he had been waiting tables and working in restaurants since he was 16 years old. He tried to catch the guy and give the hundred bucks back to him. Well, that made my eyes get a little teary. Bek's too.

As Lewis walked off, I was left with such a nice feeling about both our waiter and the customer who had tipped $100 to a waiter that hadn't even served him. I thought about how fortunate I was to witness such a cool occurrence: two nice people colliding. As I looked at my wife, and she apparently read my mind. And I'll just leave it up to your imagination as to where the second $100 came from!

ENTRÉE II

Cinderella Man

O ne of my favorite movies is *Cinderella Man*, starring
Russell Crowe. I'm pretty sure some of you ladies might
be fans of him, too. It's the true story of a heavyweight boxer
named James Braddock who lived during the depression (the
1930s) and how he uses what little money he has to feed his
wife and kids.

One day, he gets called up to a big fight. After his trainer
tapes his hands and laces on his gloves, he learns that Braddock
hasn't eaten in days. The trainer (not a waitress) goes some-
where and returns with a big bowl of hash. Braddock's mouth
is watering, and he is dying to eat, but the trainer forgot to
bring a spoon or fork and of course he has his boxing gloves
on which he can't even take off by himself. The trainer leaves
again to get silverware, but while he is gone, Braddock suffers
over the hot, delicious, and abundant food. When the trainer
finally returns, he finds the fighter with his face buried in the
bowl, hash all over him.

It's a funny part in the movie, and it shows how much he
sacrifices for his wife and children. But it's not funny when it

happens to real customers in real restaurants all over the place who are being served by careless waiters and waitresses. It's crazy, I know, but it happens. It happens even more frequently when you order from the bar.

This second entrée is about the basics of waiting on tables. A boxing trainer has an excuse to bring delicious food to the table with no silverware but trained professionals do not. Check out the following tips—the meat and potatoes of serving—and getting the job done right. These are the basic things the customer feels his 15% should include without having to ask for them.

Tip #11: The 3-Minute Rule

Get to the table ASAP. When a new customer, or customers, have been seated, be at their table immediately to greet them, especially if you're not in the middle of serving another customer. And if you are, then let the new customer know you'll be right over. On the first trip to the table take water or get drink orders to get the ball rolling. There is nothing more frustrating to a customer than sitting and waiting without being acknowledged. It actually makes people feel disrespected, which is death to a tip.

I have a friend who will get up and leave a restaurant if he goes unnoticed for three minutes after sitting at a table. These three minutes of waiting indicates many things to him, including poor service, poor staffing, and weak management. He leaves and never returns to that restaurant. So get to the table quick. Remember, there is only one chance for a first impression and the clock is ticking.

"The dictionary is the only place where success comes before work."

—Mark Twain

Tip #12: I Love This Place

Do you know how many times I ask a waitress about something on the menu and she replies, "Oh, I've never tried it?" or "I don't really like oysters" and it's an oyster bar she works at! Well, not knowing your menu or not liking the food on it is a good way to guarantee reduced tips. If you really don't like the food where you work, I highly recommended you find a restaurant where you do like the food and get a job there. Not only will this be better for you, but for the restaurant itself, not to mention the customers. Then try every dish they make. Know the menu like it's your menu (because it is). Become an aficionado on every plate.

To make sure it's not just your preferences you're pushing; do a little forensic research. Watch which meals come back with the plate clean and which end up half-touched or hiding under a napkin.

Don't be afraid to show your passion for the food when you talk to your customers about the dishes. Say, "Oh, I love the beef stew (or spaghetti and meatballs or stir fry vegetables)!" But whatever you do, avoid the lines, "I've never tried that" or "I don't like it." These are tip-reducing answers. Let's make money; not just work a shift.

Tip #13: Hit Me with Your Best Shot

Following up the previous tip, let's also look at it in the following way. I travel a lot and eat at many excellent restaurants for one time and one time only. That means I'm dining in establishments unfamiliar to me, so I always ask the waitress, "What's the most popular item on your menu?" The answers range from, "Uh, I don't know, what are you in the mood for?" to "Really, everything is good!" The thing is, there is always a number one seller in any restaurant. If you don't know what that is, it would be beneficial to both your customers and you to find out. Once you know which dish gets ordered the most (along with two or three runner-ups), you can respond to the question like you are the authority on your menu. This one tip will be a game changer. It will increase their enjoyment and your tip. Hey, and what if that meal is costlier than the salad or burger they were going to order? Well, the restaurant makes more money, and you do, too. Win win! Yeah!

Tip #14: Get It Right (please)

You don't need to be Wonder Woman or have special powers. If you can't memorize the order (and do so without mistakes), no big deal. Use a pad and a pen if you need to. You can even jot down notes to remember who gets what. Your customers don't care *how* you take their orders, or how long it takes you to write the order down; they only care that you get it right.

This is an area where I see so much room for improvement in most of the restaurants in which I've dined. Again, I've eaten at thousands of restaurants all over the world. Servers will generally get at least one thing wrong with the order. If you concentrate on this one tip alone, you will improve your take-home cash and enjoy your shift more. The "no mayonnaise" may be trivial to you, but it's usually a deal breaker to the one who is ordering.

"Wisdom is knowing what to do; virtue is doing it."

—*David Jordan*

Tip #15: Please Remember Me!

Here's one where exercising your memory muscle is going to help you score big! When you take a table's order, don't just write down each order but also remember who ordered what.

(If you don't have a good memory, devise a system of notes to help you remember.) That way you won't have to ask, "Okay, who gets the Diet Coke, who gets the unsweetened tea?" Same goes with entrees and desserts.

I know this seems like a small detail, something that shouldn't really matter, but here is how we customers perceive it:

When you took our order, you seemed so concerned and thoughtful, and you acted like you really cared. Now, three minutes later, you can't even remember what drink we ordered. We are hurt and disappointed. And, oh heavens, what about our food!

Remembering who ordered what is a practice regularly done by great waiters and waitresses all over the country. And high-tipping customers appreciate this efficiency and devotion to the trade. Yes, the honorable trade of WAITRESSING.

"The way to develop self- confidence is to do the thing you fear."

—*William Jennings Bryan*

Tip #16: Cinderella's Slipper

Cinderella forgot her slipper and our boxer's trainer forgot his fork! The same thing happens when a customer is served.

French fries without ketchup
Bread or biscuits without butter (grits too, but y'all know that)
Food of any kind without salt and pepper
Coffee without cream and sugar
Unsweetened tea without sweetener- the low-calorie style

Most all other condiments are reasonable to be asked for, but these are like silverware—or even a slipper!

"To get through the hardest journey we need take only one step at a time, but we must keep on stepping."

—*Chinese Proverb*

Tip #17: Be an Ambassador

You are the liaison between the customer and the kitchen. You play ambassador on the part of the customer, who generally isn't allowed to go into the kitchen themselves to check if their food is right. We, the hungry, can only tell you "the way" we want our food: what sides, how crispy or rare, dressing on the side, no gravy on the hamburger steak, or a severe allergy to peanuts. You write all this down or key it into the terminal, and it goes to the kitchen. But I'm sure you know your job as a liaison isn't finished at this point, not if the food comes out with gravy and dressing and peanuts all over it. Your experience has shown you that the kitchen makes mistakes, so if you don't catch it, you will have to deliver the food twice.

Here's the thing, you can fulfill your job as liaison before you even serve the food for the first time. Just take an extra five seconds to check that the food is right and just the way you asked. Unfortunately, in my experience, the waitress more often than not skips this step and brings the food to the table, and the customer has to state the obvious. I understand that a lot is required of you. You're juggling ten tables and fifteen or twenty meals. You're amazing! However, this little but important step will make you even more amazing and will make all the difference to your customers. And ultimately, it'll actually save you time in the big picture. So, run interference for your diners and double-check that your cook gets those orders right, so your customers don't have to.

Tip #18: Stand Up For Your Customers

Just as you need to be an ambassador, as the previous tip discusses, sometimes you have to stand strong and take up for your customers. Yes, apologize if the food is slow. Then go back in the kitchen and raise hell! You are the advocate for your customers. If the problem isn't remedied quickly, it's a good time to offer more bread, make sure drinks are filled, or promise a free dessert at the end of the meal. Go the extra mile quickly before your tip is eroded.

I have a favorite waitress and bartender at Baumhowers, a local chain serving hot wings and other great food, Her name is Sheila, and she is very feisty. If my wife's chicken finger salad is not ready in a timely manner, Sheila goes back to the kitchen and gives the chef a piece of her mind. We are so appreciative to her for standing up for us. We never ever have to complain or say a word. And how do we show our appreciation? Her tip goes from 20% to 50% on the spot!

Tip #19: See the Future

Yes, I know, but great waitresses see problems before they occur, like slow food! To preempt the problem of slow food, manage your customers' expectations. If you know that some entrees take the chef forever, warn your peeps before they order it. "Good choice; I love that shrimp po'boy, but it takes an extra twenty minutes. Just to let you know in case you're in a rush." They will appreciate you running defense for them. That is what I call great waitressing! And great tips will follow. I have even had waitresses give me a wink and a nod to indicate that my choice on the menu was not a good one. She never said a word, but I got the message, and she got double the tip.

Tip #20: Be a Mom

One way to be sure to tend to your tables properly is to think of each table of customers as one of your own children, one of your own babies. A mother is constantly checking on her babies. She never leaves them alone but for a few minutes. She has her ears alert for their cries. She has intuition about when they're tired or hungry.

If a table were your baby, you wouldn't walk right by and not even glance at him. You wouldn't do that to your kids (who don't even pay your bills like your customers do). Look at your customers. Smile at them. Care about them. Tell them you will be right back. That's good service. (And that's good money.)

Tip #21: Your Customer Is Watching

Check often to see if your customers' food is ready from the kitchen. There's nothing worse in a dining experience than sitting there hungry as you watch your food get cold on the kitchen window and see your waitress shooting the breeze with her amigos. Be aware that your customers see more than you may realize, and your customers are, after all, the people you're working for. They're the ones who give you raises—on a minute-by-minute basis. They are the reason you are working there. You aren't there to meet new people or be popular. If you're there to make money, work your tip, not Facebook or the nice-looking bartender.

Tip #22: I Like It Like That

If a customer asks for two bottom buns on their hamburger instead of the normal whole bun, don't let them know you think that sounds stupid. Your goal is to have happy customers who get what they request. Those are the kinds of customers who leave bigger tips. Make a weird request seem doable. "Sure thing!" (Or, if it seems appropriate, you could say something like: "Well, that's creative! We can do that!") Then follow through with the kitchen to make sure it happens. And when you deliver the food to the table: "I gotcha that double bottom burger, just like you like it!" or joke with him: "As seen on TV!" Do your job like you love it. In fact, have fun, and let yourself actually love it. Joy is rewarded with more joy (and good tips). And yes, I have seen this version of a burger ordered.

ENTRÉE III

The Secret to Men

I am really taking my life into my own hands by telling you ladies the secret inner workings of men. I am breaking the sacred trust of my own kind (all males). But remember, my goal is to help you (all waitresses) make more money, live richer, fuller lives, and feed your babies too. Lean in and listen close, and I will pull back the curtain and reveal to you how we are wired, what makes us tick, and what makes us stop ticking. I'll tell you what we like to see and hear—and what we don't. And don't let anyone (especially some guy) fool you into thinking that he is not like that. We all are! These are principles, not some fashion magazine's pop psychology. I could write volumes on these principles, but I am only going to disclose to you what you need to make more money. And hey, if you use this information to make your relationships better so be it.

The largest living thing on the earth is not the humpback whale or a grove of aspen trees in Colorado. The largest living thing in the world is, without a doubt, **the male ego**. Don't get confused or jump to conclusions and think that since it's so big that it is also solid and stable and concrete. Not only is the male ego the largest thing in the world, but it's also the most fragile. The male ego is a wonderful, powerful thing, able to achieve any amazing feat imaginable. It provides the unction for men to fight wars for freedom, to sail the seven seas, and to become experts in any and all fields. And, of course, it prevents us from stopping and asking directions when we are lost.

Now, here is the good part: Men are crazy about you. Let me put it another way: men love women! Men love waitresses. Yes, we do. And you happen to be one, right?

Like all huge living things, the male ego needs to eat a lot to stay alive, and that's where you come in. What type of food does it eat? Not the kind your restaurant sells. No. The kind of food the male ego eats is *respect!* Respect is the main course, and attention is the platter it's served upon. And that's what you sell. And the price—well, it's your tip. I'm going to show you a ton of ways to sell it and serve it.

What does the care and feeding of the male ego look like? It can be as simple as complimenting us on a new shirt, a hat or a haircut. It always entails listening to us like we are the last man on earth. The ego loves to hear waitresses laughing at its jokes or bragging on its newest purchase (trucks, cars, boats, watches). But be careful, one slip of the tongue, even if you meant no harm or you thought it was funny, and the fragile male ego will break like Humpty Dumpty.

These tips will show you how to feed and care for the male ego. But before we go there, let me take one step back because I need you to really understand something a little better. You see, all men, even a homeless man, wants his homeless woman to show him respect. Oh yes, guys "like" love, sex, sports, food and our friends. But in the same way you girls want to be loved and cherished, we men want to be shown (fed) respect. Then, and only then, do we even contemplate loving and cherishing. And big tipping! Understand?

As you read all the tips in this entrée, keep in mind the huge male ego and its fragility. Also please, please, please remember that guy could have eaten at home if it was just nourishment for the body he craved. He could have gone to a drive-thru, saved money, and not had to tip at all. But no! He chose to eat at a sit-down restaurant and pay more than food at home or a drive-thru. And guess what else? They even chose your place to eat.

So use these tips to enhance his meal, his experience, his ego—even his life. Remember, us guys get the crap knocked out of us all day at work. There are millions of us who are beaten down by demanding bosses, angry customers, even by our wife and girlfriends. We want and need a refuge. We want a place that strengthens us again and encourages us to keep fighting—fighting the world or our failing health or our crumbling finances.

Help us! We are practically begging you to be our allies, if not but for just one meal. Come running to our rescue, and most of us will return the favor very generously. The following tips will show you exactly how to do this.

"It is the province of knowledge to speak, and it's the privilege of wisdom to listen."

—Oliver Wendell Holmes

Tip #23: Be Julia Roberts

I love Julia Roberts; she's a great actress. And a good waitress is, essentially, like a good actress. In *Steel Magnolias*, Julia Roberts was soft and kind and fun. In *Erin Brockovich*, she was strong, sassy, and intelligent. It's the same person acting out different roles. And what was the main reason she played these opposite roles? Money. Yes, money, plain and simple. The more versatile an actress is, the more successful she is likely to be, and the better she will be paid. I bet you never thought of waitressing in that light. But waitresses also get higher monetary rewards for versatility.

If a waitress is the same with all types of men, she will make an average tip. If she can efficiently get a man's food to him at a decent temperature and in the right order and keep his drinks filled and ask if he needs anything else, she will certainly get her 15%. Adapt to your customers, and you stand to make far more than 15%, probably more than 30%. That's called doubling your income.

Here's what adapting to your customers might look like: If he's a guy who is a good ol' country boy, a great waitress knows how to mimic some of his characteristics and talk about pickup trucks and deer hunting. If he's the Marlboro Man type, she can adapt to the strong silent type by being softer and quieter, maybe being kinder and more serving. If the customer is a young techie from Radio Shack, she can also talk about electronics and video games.

Here's the thing: More than anything, a man wants to feel good about himself. He wants to believe that he's interesting and worthwhile, and if you can spend a little time and effort helping him feel that way, you increase your chances of raising your tip to as much as 100 to 200% of that meal. And sometimes it only takes that one customer to double your tip money for that shift.

"Put your hand on a hot stove for a minute, and it seems like an hour; sit with a pretty girl for an hour, and it seems like a minute. That's relativity."

—Albert Einstein

Tip #24: My Best Tip Yet

This tip alone is actually worth more than the price of the book. If used daily, it should earn you more than enough to buy this book every day. Yes, it's simple, but all of the greatest things in life are also simple. Are you ready? Here it is: Ask your male customer, "What kind of work do you do?" This is a tip increaser of the highest power, especially when a waitress asks a man, although it will also work to some degree with women.

When your customer answers, listen. Yes, just listen. It sounds simple, but this is the most crucial part, and it's the one many people forget to do. Men (the male ego) love to be listened to. We also love to hear things like, "Oh! Wow! Really? Cool!"

Oh yeah, one more thing, the ego hates to be interrupted. Some women have got this down to a science with their boyfriends, but few do it with their income providers (customers). Customers will actually pay you to listen. Try this tip, and watch *your* tips increase.

Tip #25: Keep This Tip to Yourself

Now, this one is almost too powerful to share with you because you will have men wrapped around your pinky finger. And if it were used on me, I would be prone to shell out a huge tip myself, so don't spread this one around.

After you learn your customer's occupation, as the last tip instructed, you lean over to the man or group of men and say, "Could I ask your advice on a subject?" If they are lawyers, ask about divorce; if they are doctors, ask about your sick son. Tailor your questions to the man or men sitting at your table and then sit back and watch the male ego get larger and larger. "Oh! Wow! Really? Cool!"

Tip #26: A Hamburger for the Ego

You can use this tip as an alternate follow-up to learning what your customer does for a living. After you know his occupation, show further interest by asking questions about it. "How did you get a career in _____?" Or: "I've never met someone who does_____. What's it like?" And then do a little more active listening. "Oh! Wow! Really? Cool!"

> *"The recipe for perpetual ignorance is: Be satisfied with your opinions and content with your knowledge."*
>
> —*Elbert Hubbard*

Tip #27: Just a Touch Pays So Much

This tip is for those times when a man is alone at your table, and you've already engaged him in conversation. If he tells you a story or a joke, or anything that's important to him, be sure to wait until he's finished. (This is just as important as making sure his food is hot or that his order is right.) When he has finished with his joke or story, respond generously with the appropriate emotional reaction. Laugh or say, "Wow," or even cry if you're moved. Then, and here's the kicker, just touch him on the shoulder as you walk away. That, girl, will pay dividends!

A word of caution: You will have to use your own judgment with each customer as to what degree of contact is appropriate. And certainly take into account whether the man has come into your restaurant with his wife or girlfriend. Like I said, this if for when a man is alone. All I know is that this move (tip) works like crazy, and waitresses have told me that this is their best money maker.

Tip #28: I Love That Name

If you have a customer come in who has his name on his shirt, he's giving you a leg up on a huge tip increaser. Because guess what? His name is either your favorite name or you have a brother with that name or an old boyfriend with that name, or you've just always liked that name. Keep it true, but find something you like about it, and tell him so. If you do this, believe me, he will double whatever he was going to tip you. Why? Because you have just made his life a little bit better, even if just for a half hour. Enhance his meal, and he will reward you. Enhance his life, and the reward gets even bigger.

Tip #29: Are You a Real Cowboy?

Imagine that a male customer at one of your tables is wearing a cowboy hat. This is a perfect opportunity to stroke the male ego. I don't care if he's 2 years old or 92, you will increase your tip if you ask him one question: "Are you a real cowboy?" If you want your regular tip, just keep on doing what you've been doing. If you want a new dishwasher, then remember your innate power over men and ask that cowboy-hat-wearing man this one question. Try it!

Tip #30: We are Just Big Kids

I'll let you in on a secret: You know all guys had a mom, and you know we all love our mom in one way or another, but maybe you don't know that most of us guys still like to be mommied every now and then. Try a little role-playing. Yes, I have seen many great waitresses put on "the Mom." They say, "Ah, poor baby. You want some more coffee?" or "I love to see a hungry man eat." Come on "Julia," you can do it!

Tip #31: Sneaky Tip

Keep an eye out for lapel pins. People display the things that are important to them. If you spot a lapel pin, do not miss the opportunity to ask about it. "That's a nice pin. What does it stand for?" Then go ahead, let 'em talk and remember, "Oh! Wow! Really? Cool!" (Note, the same applies hats and shirts with logos. As they talk, their wallets get looser and looser. And you know what that leads to....)

Tip #32: Let Us In

This tip is for the quiet ones among you. You've got to give up a little to get a little. Let the customer in. Yes, let them know just a little bit about you by finding common ground. If he has four kids at the table, you might say, "I have kids the same age" (only if you do). To make this task easier, you can wear a name tag or a pin with your kitty on it or you might comment on his hat or mustache or whatever it is that will help you open up a little and connect with your customer. Personally, I give better tips to single moms with six kids based solely on their need, even if they're not spectacular waitresses. But you've got to let your customers know you a little to allow this to happen. (Caution: You will need to use your own judgment about what to tell which customers and when.) But don't dump on them. Remember, it's all about them.

Tip #33: Are You Kidding Me?

Men love to hear these phrases, so use them to feed that large ego. Yes, they are simple, but they uplift that beaten down man I have been telling you about. Make these words your *income-producing* words.

1. Amazing!!!

2. You're so right.
3. Wow! That made my day.
4. That's totally awesome!!
5. Wow! That sounds great!
6. You can say that again!
7. How did you know that? (Guys, in particular, like to show women how much they know. So this line is a huge pat on the back.)
8. Take me with you. (It's said jokingly when your customer tells you about a great trip he's going on.)
9. You and me both, brother.
10. I would love to do that.
11. Are you kidding me?
12. I wish I could do that! (When your customer talks about waterskiing or woodworking or writing a book; it doesn't matter what!)
13. I feel you.
14. Don't I know it!

Tip #34: Watcha' Reading?

I know that you think that the guy who orders a cup of coffee and opens a book is going to keep your table tied up for hours and tip you 50 cents or a dollar, but you have the power to change that. No, not by asking him to leave or staring him down until he does, but something much kinder to him and more profitable for you.

I have read hundreds of books in restaurants and cafes and have seen others do the same. Only a couple of times has the waitress done the smart thing, the profitable thing. Here's what she did. She asked, "Watcha reading?" or "Is that a good book?"

Do this, and the man's heart will burst with affection, and he will gladly tell you what the book is about. He'll also be more likely to lay down a five or ten when he leaves. Not bad for a cup of joe!

Tip #35: Don't Rock the Jukebox

Men are attention junkies. They know when you're checking your phone or singing to the music being played in the restaurant. This is disrespect in all men's eyes. You know this because your man hates for you to check Facebook while you are eating or watching TV with him. So please, for the sake of your tips, give us 100% of your attention. By the way, this works for relationships too. Allan Jackson told listeners not to Rock the Jukebox, meaning not to play rock and roll songs. He wanted to "hear some Jones" (George, of course). What I'm saying is, don't be more interested in the music of your restaurant than your customer. This is not a place to party; it's a place to work. I see too many waitresses involved in their own lives and their own entertainment and not their customer's.

Face your customers head on, not turned at an angle. This shows respect, as well as acceptance and receptivity. It will help put your customer at ease and let him know he doesn't have to work to get or keep your attention. Feed the ego!

Tip #36: Take a Knee

Years ago, at self-improvement seminars, I got several chances to hear Zig Ziglar speak. Over the years, Zig became one of the most honored and respected in his field. And you know what Zig's signature move was? He would kneel down on one knee on the stage, just at the right moment, to make his point or to show appreciation for his audience. It was probably just his way of showing respect. Remember, the male ego eats respect and attention. And believe me, when a waitress takes a knee at the table, there is no better way to say I'm giving you (my

customer) my full attention and respect. And, as you know by
now, money will follow.

Tip #37: It's your Show

Yes, it's your show, and you're the one up on the stage. That's
it. For every shift you work, your restaurant or café is the stage,
and you are the Julia Roberts. Since it's you in the spotlight,
remember Tip #10 that you're in business for yourself. Does
any of that make you rethink how you might act while you're
working or how you do your hair, makeup, or fingernails? You
may not think it matters at all, but to all of us men out here,
it matters!

I see waitresses out at night on the town all the time, and
you know what, I hardly recognize them. They have prettier
hair and lipstick; they look killer. All the guys in the world ask,
"Why don't they look like that at work?" You see, it goes back
to that respect thing that I told you that the ego lives on. Guys
see it as disrespect if you don't give us your best. I know that's
ridiculous, but I told you I would tell the truth. So there you
have it. Give us your best smile, your best appearance, your
best tone of voice. You know why? Because it's your stage. It's
your business. Give us the best you've got if you want our best
tip. You gotta bring it!

> *"Motivation is what gets you started; habit is what
> keeps you going."*
>
> —*Jim Rohn*

::SIDE ORDERS::

Tip #38: A Picture is Worth a Thousand Words

Another way to let your customers know who you are is to wear a pin or a locket with a picture of your children. Or if you don't have kids, wear a picture of your pet or perhaps a pin that says, "I love my dog!" or "I love my cat!" This will start lots of conversations. The more your customers know you, the more they'll care about you or feel connected to you. And they'll want to show this by tipping you well. They'll also be more apt to become repeat customers. (People like to eat where they feel comfortable and welcomed.)

"The shortest way to do many things is to do only one thing at once."

—Samuel Smiles

Tip #39: I Wanna Talk!

Ask your customers their opinion of the food. "How was your burger?" Let 'em talk, even if it's negative. Man's greatest purpose and urge is to express himself. His suggestions may better the café or even your performance. And he is liable to tip you just for listening.

"Never argue with stupid people; they will drag you down to their level and then beat you with experience."

—*Mark Twain*

Tip #40: The Grass Is Always Greener

If you have a couple at your table (a man and woman who are together), and they seem to be in a good mood, here's something you can do to charm them. First, look at their ring fingers. If they're married, say to him, "Is this your girlfriend?" or say to both, "Are you two boyfriend and girlfriend?" Now, why do this when you know they're married? Because, in some way, everyone wants to be what they're not. People yearn for the greener grass on the other side of the fence. Doing what I suggest here will give this couple that greener grass, if only for the evening.

When the couple answers that they're not dating, they're married, you say, "Oh, you two looked so happy and in love, I thought you were on a date!" Now, if you see no wedding rings, do the exact opposite. "Is this your lovely wife?" When the answer comes that they're not married, you tell them, "Oh, you two looked so perfect together; I thought you were a happily married couple."

Tip #41: Let's Work Together

You know how the management wants you to upsell? Maybe more drinks or an appetizer or dessert? Well, that works not just in the restaurant's favor, but also in yours. Work that check up, and you work your tip up, right? Funny how so many things that are good for the restaurant are also good for you. Your boss is not your opposition; you're actually on the same team!

Tip #42: Ninja Selling

This is brilliant. I've only seen it once, and it worked. After everyone at our table refused the dessert offered by our waitress, she said, "May I suggest our pie to take home; it's delicious! You can eat it later for a snack; that's what I do." Cha-ching for you and for the restaurant.

Tip #43: An Added Extra

Here's an easy bonus you can throw in for an extra dollar or two added to your tip: "Would you like a to-go cup for your drink?" I love this idea, and I tip it. Others do, too.

Tip #44: You've Got a TV at Home

If you work in a bar or restaurant with a television, you'll have to train yourself to ignore it. I get it; it's hard to not to be sucked in, especially if your home team is playing. Just be sure to record or TiVo it so you can watch it later (not at work). You can even playfully tell your customer not to tell you the score. But whatever you do, don't turn your back on your customer so you can watch the TV. Remember that sign around their neck (Make me feel important)? Keep your focus on your customer, which is equal to keeping your mind on your money and your money on your mind!

Tip #45: Hold the Pine-Sol, Please

Have you ever sat in a café or restaurant (as a customer) and had someone come out and start mopping up all around you? Maybe they even asked you to pick up your feet while you were still eating? Did the smell of Pine-Sol or the sound of a roaring vacuum enhance your meal?

Understandably, 24/7 restaurants have no other time to clean than when they're open to diners. But most places are only open for so many hours a day. If it's your job to clean, come in early or stay late and do it when no one is eating. If it's someone else's job, do whatever you've got to do to protect your customers' dining experience (and your tip). We will love you for it.

"Bad habits are easier to abandon today than tomorrow."

—Yiddish Proverb

Tip #46: Word Power

Your words (anyone's) are the most powerful moneymaker you possess. Use them wisely, and use them well. Make your customers feel good about themselves; help lift their spirits and self-esteem. You have the power to turn someone's bad day into a good one. Take this part of your job seriously (and do it with true authenticity), and it will reap the rewards. Besides, making someone else feel good it will also make you feel good. It's a win-win every time.

Tip #47: Uniforms Look Smart

Ever know a guy who wasn't much to look at until one day he comes walking in wearing a military uniform. Wow, what an improvement. He not only appears more attractive but smarter, too, right? Yes, and the same thing occurs when you wear a sharp or cute uniform. You look smarter, more diligent, more about doing your profession. And the customer immediately believes you must know what you're doing. The customer then relaxes and believes in you. All of this happens when you dress for the part you are playing. And believe it or not, people tip "professionals" more than they do amateurs. Hey, if you have to go buy your own uniform, and if the boss doesn't mind; I'll bet Amazon will ship you one today.

> *"In the absence of clearly-defined goals, we become strangely loyal to performing daily trivia until ultimately we become enslaved by it."*
>
> —*Robert Heinlein*

Tip #48: Costumes are Better

Yes, you read that right; costumes are even better than uniforms. Costumes, especially those that go with the style of the restaurant, are very tipish. They do everything the uniform does, but they add the mystery, the fantasy, and the fun! Show me a waitress in a pirate costume or orange shorts and tied up tee shirts, and I'll show you higher tips than someone wearing street clothes. Let's make money!

Tip #49: You're No Waitress

That's right! Don't think of yourself as just a waitress. No! You're not just an order taker and a drink refiller. You, my friend, are an Experience Enhancer, so learn to act like what you truly are.

Tip #50: How Do You Know?

How do you know if you're doing a good job? There are lots of clues. How many times did they have to ask for things you should have thought of beforehand? Did you get them talking? Did you get their orders right? (That's a big one) And one last clue: Did they say goodbye? If not, did they leave a good tip?

If the answer is no to any of these questions, go back and study these tips. Make yourself the best waitress you can be, and the money will follow.

Tip #51: Giving Back

Consider showing your appreciation to your best repeat customers with a gift. Even a simple handwritten thank-you card would touch many people's hearts. This shows how grateful you are for that customer's repeat business and loyalty. Believe me, this is how people build their businesses, and you are in business too, right? Giving back is a principle that will always work! Be a giver.

> *"Feeling gratitude and not expressing it is like wrapping a present and not giving it."*
>
> —*William Arthur Ward*

::DESSERT::

The Awesome Power of a Waitress

Y ou may not know that this is my first book. Oh, it's not that I haven't written poems and songs and given speeches and even eulogies. I had for so long wanted to write a book but was, of course, afraid of failure. I could just hear my critics saying, "What does Joel (me) know about being a waitress?" He has never even waited a table. Heck, dude, you're not even female.

It was at this low point that a wonderful girl just like one of you said something that changed me. Her words seemed to reach inside of me and rearranged my internal furniture. I had, by this time, read thousands of self-help books and been to seminars all over the place. I had accomplished many things but never written a book; especially, about waitresses.

What did she say? What could she have said that I hadn't read or learned or even taught others? I was a 50-year-old man, and she was a 22-year-old waitress. What the heck did she know?

I need to give you a little background before I tell you what she said. You see, she had watched me build my auto glass business from a one-man business to one of the largest in the area. She had seen me accomplish many goals just by her observing nature. So here are the words. She said, "You know what; everybody here thinks you can do anything you set your mind to." One stinking sentence. One waitress. One life changed—mine.

As she walked off, I remembered all of the antics I had come up with in my auto glass business to double our sales every year. We used crazy idea after crazy idea to attract and please our customers. I taught my team what to do, what to say, and when to say them. I taught them how to make our customers feel important and how to make them feel good about themselves and our business. I taught my people to go the extra mile in everything we did and in how we did it.

What happened? It made our customers so crazy loyal they would go to extremes to do business with us. They traveled unreasonable distances (passing right by many of our competitors), and they argued with their insurance companies saying they would use us or cancel their policies. These customers were constantly sending me cards and letters and leaving me voicemails telling me how great our windshield business was. Our installers and office people made tip after tip from wow-ed customers. Now I ask you, when was the last time you tipped the person who repaired your car?

As I pondered all this, I finally realized that not only had I not ever waited a table, but I had also never personally replaced a windshield, either. Go figure. So I started writing.

My First Cup of Coffee

No, this is stronger and harsher than coffee. This is like three shots of espresso with no water, milk, or sugar. But it's time for this book to end, and I want to leave you with my best. I have to tell it like it is if I have any hopes of being any help to you. This last cup of coffee is a culmination of many, if not all, of these tips. And it is not only true about waitressing, but it's also true in every other area of life. Ready? Here it is: "You get what you deserve." That's it. As waitresses or students or salesmen or athletes or whatever we are—*we all get what we deserve!*

I hate to be so blunt but its one of those harsh realities of life, and I can't change it. All I know is that it's a principle of life, and you can choose to abide by it or not, but believe me, you can't change it.

I, truly from my heart, want this book to change your life. I want your life to be richer and fuller with more happiness and more success. Not only for you, the waitress, but also for your family and all involved. But I can't change it for you.

Believe me, if I could, I would, but life doesn't work like that. No one can change your life (or tip income) but you. I pray you do!

> *"Inaction breeds doubt and fear. Action breeds confidence and courage. If you want to conquer fear, do not sit home and think about it. Go out and get busy."*
>
> *—Dale Carnegie*

My Last Cup of Coffee

Much of this book was written in restaurants and cafés. And I owe a huge debt of gratitude to all of the waitresses who poured and re-poured my coffee and asked how I was doing or whether I needed anything. I am especially grateful to those of you who asked, "Whatcha writin'?" This book is for you and for waitresses everywhere.

As I savor my last few sips, I think about all the people being served by millions of waitresses all over this country and how you ladies are being the gift of joy or solace or companionship to your customers. What an incredible job you have. You get to make people happy! I know of no more important work than that. It is my hope that you recognize the significance of what you bring to people and that you take pride in this part of your job as never before.

When you follow the tips in this book, you will realize that making people feel happy and better about themselves makes for bigger tips and everyone wins: the customer, the restaurant, the management, and, most importantly, you! It's a positive cycle all started by you, the waitress. If I haven't yet had the pleasure of sitting at your particular table, and I haven't had the honor of tipping you, I hope to get that chance one day soon.

"If we did all the things we are capable of, we would literally astonish ourselves."

—Thomas Edison

Joel loves to hear your waitress tips, stories and comments, so please contact him at joelbrowngolf@yahoo.com.

Joel is also available for workshops and speaking engagements.